1

BarbaraDiane.com

ISBN: 978-0-615-93197-5

Ordering Information: Quantity sales, special discounts are

available on quantity purchases by corporations, associations

and others. For details contact admin@barbaradiane.com

BarbaraDiane.com

DEDICATION:

To my mom Sharon. Through all your struggles raising our family by yourself. You never gave up on me. Thank you for your guidance and wisdom. Your strength, bravery and grace shines through and I am forever grateful to you for helping me become who I am today.

To my parents-in-law Bud and Debbie Herndon. Your love and support has been the backbone to Brad and I through really difficult times. We wouldn't be where we are without you. Thank you for loving me like your own daughter and sharing with me some of my favorite memories ever!

Abel, Destiny, James and Isaac. Each of you have brought something different to my life for me to smile about and to learn from. Thank you for your unconditional love and forgiveness. You are the reason that I go after my dreams to show you that yours are absolutely possible. I am truly grateful to have the honor to be your mom.

My first love Brad. There isn't anyone else I would rather go through life with than you. Thank you for giving me your best and helping me grow into the woman I am. Your unconditional and forever love is a gift each day. You are my best friend, my favorite, my hero!

To my Heavenly Father. You are the reason that I sing. Thank you for seeing me through my darkest times and always having open arms. Thank you for second chances to do better. This book is for you. You are my safe place to rest, my comforter, my everything.

Testimonials:

"Rarely do you find someone who is willing to open themselves up by exposing the highs and lows of his or her life. Barbara was able to find peace and happiness despite the trials that she has faced. She takes a practical approach with affirming quotes and action steps that can easily be implemented by anyone. This was a thoroughly enjoyable read which I found identifiable and at points brought a tear to my eye."
- Ross Wilson, Scotland

"Why Your Life Sucks is like a manual for living a great life... one filled with love, happiness and success. Barbara's life stories will touch you at the core. Her openness is brave and her persistence is admirable. Follow her action steps and your life will not suck anymore!
At times I felt like crying and by the next chapter I was yelling "Way to go!" Yet through the storytelling, I found so many comparisons to my own emotional challenges. Not only does Barb point out what was wrong with her life, but she gives actionable steps to going from a life that sucks to a life that's filled with love, happiness and success."
Tracy Matthewman, Canada - TracyMatthewman.com

"Barbara's book is not only motivating and inspiring, it it full of faith and feeling! She makes the reader feel as though they are there with her through her incredible journey and also that you are not alone in yours. This book is perfect for people that feel that they are stuck in " limbo" or a " standstill" in their personal or business life. She has amazing and attainable advice that anyone can relate too. Reading this book opened my heart and my mind. I am sure it will do the same for the next reader!" Kelly Ferguson, North Carolina

"The minute I started to read WYLS I knew that it was truly written from the heart. Barbara creates a bond with you and gently kicks that amazing butt of yours into action; she lays out some simple yet deep digging "to-do's" required in order for you to take control in creating the life that you want and deserve! Thank you Barbara!"
Nicole Raza, Canada - www.newdirectionshypnosis.com

"*Why Your Life Sucks* is a gem, as is Barbara Diane! She desires nothing more than to bring you to the point of realizing your dreams, while removing the fear so that you can pursue them passionately. She is firm yet compassionate. She holds nothing back and uses her own vulnerable, powerful life experiences, and gives you action steps to put into motion what you have learned. Read this book if you are seeking clarity and are serious about making that change to propel your life forward in a powerful way."

- Amber Duncan, Washington

FOREWORD:

When I met Barb I knew immediately she had something special to share with the world. She is a strong woman who has taken her struggles in life and turned them into blessings. Through this book she is giving a step by step guide to living your best life. It is a beautiful miracle when a person can be humble enough to share their stumbling blocks in life with the world in order to make life a little better for those willing to put the work in. Barb shows you exactly how to live your best life not only through her life stories but by getting you to look inward and evaluate why your life "sucks."

I am a better person for reading this book. I am an even better person for having this woman in my life as my kindred spirit. And within these pages, you too will be able to connect with the author, my friend, Barb. I pray you will learn to better understand yourself, your purpose and through the exercises provided, make your way toward your own best life. It all starts with here. Enjoy the journey.

Blessings.

Stacey Brown - believeinhairapy.blogspot.com/

Why Your Life Sucks

I consider it a positive obligation to share the struggles and challenges that I have faced and how I got through them. These obstacles have taught me very important lessons that I needed to learn and might not have if it weren't for the circumstances I found myself in. They were painful and heartbreaking, but I am grateful for them. I look at this book as my responsibility to help those out there who choose to read this to be more fulfilled and gain clarity while moving along in life. Finding the motivation to write this book was a long time coming. I often told myself, "Who would want to listen to anything I have to say?" or "Who am I to think I can actually help people?" That voice has been silenced. I now know that

those thoughts were lies and that we all have a voice that can help someone else. I truly believe that the purpose of participating in the battles we fight is to be freed from our own challenges and then to help others be liberated as well.

I can't take credit for the miraculous things that have happened in my life or the outcomes of some of those devastating situations. When we are hopeless and at risk of losing everything, we are often saved when it seems we shouldn't be.

I admit that I don't know how God works. When I think I have Him all figured out and can read what He is doing in my life, it pretty much never works out that way. What I do know is that He is good, and He is good *all* the time. Our lives would be in a worse place if not for His unwavering power and unconditional love. It takes the ultimate trust and faith to walk with Him daily. He never forces us to do anything. He is available to those who steadily call on Him for help.

Throughout my life I have found myself asking questions like, "How did I end up here?" "Why do I feel like this?" "What am I supposed to learn from this?" and "Man! Why is this stage of my life such crap?"

I finally silenced that harsh inner critic and put the lessons I have learned into this book. Some lessons came for free and some cost me multiple thousands of dollars. I never thought I would write a book, but that annoying inkling of a feeling to get it done was too strong. I have learned that a tiny whisper is a very powerful motivator. It need not be overlooked but rather, obeyed.

Here is my disclaimer: You may LOVE or HATE this book. This book is not for everyone and is certainly not meant to please anyone. It is for those people that are searching to better themselves, their lives and their future. This book is not meant to point fingers at your own life but rather to give you a different perspective on aspects of your life that you already know you want to change. I am not going to sugar coat anything because that really doesn't help anyone. I am bold, firm, unafraid and yet compassionate, loving and understanding.

My hope for you after reading this book is that you will find the strength to get through whatever you may be facing right now; that you will walk away feeling truly valued and that this world needs to hear your voice; that you will begin to dream those dreams again and watch them become your reality. I want you to heal from the past that might have cut and hurt you so deeply. I want you to be free so that you can in turn free those around you.

As you read parts of my story and the journey I have been through, I want you to feel encouraged that if I can get through the challenges and excruciating times then you can too.

ONE

Starting Out

In my early twenties I was 'supposed' to be the happiest a person could be. I was married and had started our family. My life looked like it was going to be exactly how *I* planned it. But I couldn't figure out why I felt that my life sucked. I mean this in a way that I was missing the *'I love my life and I want to jump out bed to get the day started'* kind of feel factor that I thought my husband, beautiful babies, and cute little newly bought house would bring. I was trying to figure out why I felt unsettled deep down.

15

On the outside I was a busy young mom. Going to the gym was my hobby and outlet. We went to church, our marriage was fun and loving with a thriving and healthy intimate life. Our every need was met and nothing was really 'wrong'—but something was still missing. It's not like I woke up every day and said, "Man! My life sucks!"

Instead, it was almost like a whisper that you trick yourself into saying you didn't hear because it was so faint. I would just stop every once in a while and think, "Is this ALL there is to my life? Changing diapers, refilling sippy cups, replaying and capturing baby movies, cooking dinner and repeating the next day?" The mundaneness of serving little people was hardly a glamorous lifestyle. I thought my life would look a little prettier and exciting—but it wasn't. Then those thoughts would come to an abrupt halt when I would be startled by a death scream and need to rescue pinched little fingers from the cupboards, kiss boo-boos, tell someone to stop playing in the toilet or wipe down a jelly-smeared highchair.

Many times in our lives we don't even realize what's wrong or are able to put our finger on the issue. This book is meant to lift you up so that you can soar up to your highest potential. You'll be able to straighten out all the little kinks in your life and recognize when something is just 'off.'

There are always going to be challenges in our lives. Don't get down on yourself when those challenges come your way. They will come no matter what. It's a part of life. The problem that we need to solve when we are approached with these obstacles is how to deal with them. Throughout this book I am going to share personal stories with you—very personal stories. The point of sharing these anecdotes is so that I may open myself up to you in order to show you that you are not alone in whatever you are going through. This world loves reality, hence the reason why reality TV is all the rage. We love to see inside people's lives and discover what's *really* going on. So I will be getting really real and raw with you.

Maybe my stories will be different from yours, or perhaps they'll be exactly the same. But the point is that I have gone through bitterness, resentment, anger, hopelessness and deep suicidal thoughts. By opening up to you and being genuine about what I went through, I hope to show you that you are not alone.

My life sucked. On the outside, it probably looked normal to others. But on the inside I was anxious, fearful, and full of worry and discontentment. I am a Christian, though. I thought Christians didn't struggle with all of these miserable feelings I was having. Or at least, we weren't supposed to, right? I had Jesus, so what else mattered?

I was happily married to my best friend, and we had awesome and super fun kiddos—but I was empty. I didn't know exactly how to change that feeling or what to do or even how to get to where I wanted. But by studying other people (who I wanted to be like and who I would run like hell from) I have learned how to get from point A (unexcited about my life) to point B (being in love with my life and at peace with where I am at in every season).

I ask only for a few things before you continue reading. Take off your ego and pride. I mean that I want you to open yourself up. There is always something to learn, and if you think you have it all together, then this book isn't for you and I respectfully say you should put it down right now. I don't want you to waste your time reading something that you won't get anything out of. There is a reason you picked up this book. There may be things that you read in this book that might ruffle your feathers. Please keep an open mind and heart to what you will learn. I truly believe that when we learn certain life skills that our parents unknowingly forgot to teach us, the best can come out of every situation. I wasn't taught certain things growing up, and now I am sharing what I eventually learned.

Let me first start by saying that I am so excited for you! You are exactly who I love to connect with—people who are sick of the mundane and know that more of everything is available. I can already tell that you are passionate about life and that you deeply want to become the best version of yourself. You see your weaknesses and are searching for how to overcome them quickly. It may be easier than you think to live the life that you have dreamt of everyday. This is a no-fluff book. I will tell it like it is and I mean it.

TWO

Misery

Growing up in poverty while surviving on food stamps and other forms of assistance was humiliating. I thought something was wrong with my family and me and that God was mad at us. I HATED being poor. I felt shamed and embarrassed.

When I was about ten years old, I walked two blocks to the grocery store while living in Elmhurst, Illinois. After grabbing the things on my list, I waited in the checkout line. Behind me were two teenage boys. I could tell that they were the rambunctious sort and hoped, wished and prayed that they had for gotten something and would need to leave the line—but they didn't. After my things were rung up, I ripped a $10 food stamp out of the booklet. My total was $5.12. I was trying to figure out how much change I could give the cashier so that I could make it easier for him to make the change quickly and smoothly. Instead of an easy transaction, it was the exact opposite. The boys behind me were messing around and calling out what I needed for change and saying number after number to confuse me. I was almost to the point of tears. The cashier held up the $10 food stamp and yelled out, "Change for food stamps!" I was completely mortified and I wanted the ground to swallow me whole to get rid of me once and for all. I was finally able to make it out of the store but the wholeness as a little girl broken. I was carrying so much burden, confusion and humiliation. I hated that my family had to be so different.

I was confused about why life had to be so hard. In church we would praise an awesome God. He didn't seem so great to me. I was angry that my mom and my dad separated when I was only 6 and then divorced years later. I was resentful that we lived in poverty all of my young life. I was embarrassed that I had five siblings and a single mom. I felt ashamed that we were a Christian family, albeit a separated one. I was angry and bitter about decisions that they had made, which were completely out of my control and that would change my life forever. I was so hurt beyond belief that I didn't know how to even verbalize or express what was going on.

I was homeschooled up until I was in 5th grade. Finally, I begged my mom to send me to school. I loved the idea of tests and of having a schedule to follow. When I got to school I was the 'new girl.' It wasn't as hard to fit in and to make new friends as I had originally thought. However, I hated the feeling that I was different. I knew that my family's situation wasn't like any of the other kids'. I could see it on their faces. I would wake up worried and go to bed worried. I was embarrassed to say that my mom and dad weren't together anymore and that I had more siblings than most other families all together. My clothes were faded, worn and passed down. I dreaded my mom picking me up because our car was loud and rusty. I was so ashamed of who I was. Although I had no control over my life's circumstances at the age of 11, I tried to wear a smile, show confidence and hope that my circumstances at home wouldn't be uncovered.

When I was in 8th grade we moved from the Chicago area to Baltimore. I didn't know anyone there, but I was excited to start a new life in which no one would know what my family had gone through.

I used to be bitter about and angry that other people could just have what they needed, go on vacations, buy new clothes and drive cars that wouldn't break down. It was so confusing to me. I wanted to figure it out. I wanted to be one of *them* when I grew up. It seemed like *those* people had figured something out that I hadn't. They knew the answers to life that we didn't have. I was determined to figure it out.

I used to get so mad at God and ask him, "Why was I born into this family? Why couldn't I have different parents who stayed together and who took better care of me?" I didn't understand why I was a mangy little girl that walked around feeling insecure, afraid and anxious. I felt so different and odd while growing up.

While living in Maryland, my life actually seemed more normal than it had ever been. My sister and brother's old friends from Texas had started a church in Maryland. They would have friends over to hang out, and I got to be the one to observe all of the cool people.

Brad was the family friend who was always at our house to hang out with my older brother and sister. For an 8th grader, I felt pretty cool to be allowed to tag along. Throughout the years, Brad became a really solid friend to me. He was someone who I could trust and get advice from; he even gave me home-work help. He was always mature in the way he carried himself and I felt comfortable enough to get his advice, even about guys from school. I knew that he loved me like a little sister and cared a lot for me as his friend. I was very grateful for his friendship; he was a true companion and I knew we would stay connected no matter where we ended up in our lives.

My mom remarried when I was 16. I felt alone—*very* alone. At such a critical time in my life, I once again felt aban-doned. It seemed as if I had no one in my corner to comfort my heartache and wipe away my painful tears. My life had changed drastically again due to someone else's decision. It was confus-ing. I had a difficult time understanding and processing my emotions. It sucked. I didn't know how to communicate to my mom how painful it was for me when she remarried. Before her new marriage, it was only my mom, brothers, sisters and myself surviving together. When someone else came into the picture, everything shifted. Walls were forming very sturdily around my heart due to this new pain and loneliness. I was determined that no one would ever see past those walls that hid the emptiness I was feeling. Instead, I kept up a smiling façade and feigned confidence.

In the summer before my junior year of high school, I was in Myrtle Beach on a weeklong leadership retreat. We went out to go Go-Carting one of those nights with a small group of people. During that time, I was learning how to drive manual transmission on Brad's Eclipse. It was so much fun! As I came to the intersection on the way to the Go-Cart place, the light turned red and I froze. I was sitting in the middle of the inter-section and didn't know what to do. Brad yelled urgently, "Get out of the road! GO!" I was stunned out of fear that I could have gotten us in an accident and because of the way he yelled at me. I felt like he was so angry with me. I had never heard him raise his voice or even get upset for that matter. I let him down and it crushed me.

When we got to the Go-Cart place, I was numb. I let my emotions get the best of me and I shut down. I was quietly hurt-ing and didn't know how to work it out. I wanted Brad to know that I was hurt by the way he reacted but I didn't want to open up and let him in. As we got out of the car, Brad said he was sorry. That was it—"I'm sorry." My only response was "Oh, it's okay." That was all, but I still felt like that tiny conversation wasn't good enough. I still needed more time to process what just happened.

Later that night, we got a chance to talk a little more. Brad apologized repeatedly for acting the way he did, and he told me how badly he felt for making me cry. He told me that he really cared about my life. As he opened up to me, I felt so loved (in a completely platonic, nonromantic way). He actually cared enough about me to apologize to me. Brad told me, "You are the most beautiful girl on the inside, and I love your heart. You are my best friend and I would never do anything to hurt you. I am so honored to be as close to you as I am." He told me how excited he was to see what I did with my life and who I would become. I had never felt so unconditionally valued as a human being or cared for.

That crazy and confusing night turned out to be one of my greatest. It was that week that I heard God's audible voice say, "You are going to marry him." For the first time in my life, I clearly trusted what God had spoken to me. I believed that voice without a doubt and realized Brad was breaking down the walls that I had spent years building. Brad was able to show me what it meant to be honored and appreciated. He probably didn't even realize the magnitude of his kindness and what it meant to me.

Brad and I got married three months after I graduated high school. I was just shy of my 19th birthday and we lived in a community style of living with 17 of our closest friends. We sold all our belongings to live a plain life. I guess we were trying to model Acts 2:45 which says, "They sold whatever they owned and pooled their resources so that each person's need was met." (The Message Version) Our entire group of friends quickly saved up and bought 52 acres in Gassaway, West Virginia. The goal was to be able to build separate house for everyone on the land and live a simple lifestyle. There were three other married couples and the others in the group were single. The couples each had their our own bedroom and the singles shared the loft —one side for the ladies and the other for the guys. I was young, married and blissfully in love that at the time nothing else mattered.

The *bliss* quickly wore off. Our daily life was quite boring and unproductive. I would go to bed late and wake up late. I had no passion or drive for anything. None of the girls worked outside the home, just the guys would work *if* and *when* they had any. I felt lazy and like my spirit was dying. My life revolved around getting laundry done (for everyone who lived on the land) and cooking dinner which was no small feat. It was exhaustingly boring. Our home, or 'hay house' (as we called it). It was made out of hay. No joke. The inside walls were covered by drywall with stacks of hay that were plastered in concrete. The designers of this house were crafty and creative.

Although we lived a simple lifestyle, money was slim— and that was a generous statement. In Gassaway, West Virginia, there isn't much to thrive on. The initial dream for this land idea was not Brad's nor mine but rather belonged to a friend of ours. We were not forced, but rather went along freely with it. We had looked up to and admired this person. Our group of friends were young and there wasn't much holding us back from pursuing this. Some would say we were a cult because of our way of living. I take full responsibility and don't blame anyone else for that adventurous and strange period of my life.

Brad and I quickly became pregnant with our first son after we got married. I knew I was supposed to be over the moon. But I wasn't. In fact, I was the complete opposite. I was depressed and thought of suicide every day. *Was this it?* I asked myself. *Would I die here living a meaningless life?* It sure felt like that and I hated it. My life sucked. At 19 years old this was not how I wanted to live our life together. The purpose of living out this lifestyle was to be close with God and find the real meaning of life. I assumed it was bad to be part of the 'real world' since we were trying to escape it. It felt as if we figured out something that everyone else was blinded to. I was a follower and so ignorant of God's truth for my life. And the thing is, I never felt further from God. I was filled with loneliness, sadness and depression. And I thought that he literally forgot about me. After all, I was in the mountains of Gassaway for crying out loud!

I felt like I was too useless to love. Why would anyone find anything lovable about me, especially in those circumstances? I remember driving on the highway in a little red truck. I had my hand on the handle. If I just opened the door while going 65 mph, I might be able to end my life right then and there. As miserable as I was with our lifestyle (not because we didn't have a lot of money, but because I was dying mentally, spiritually and emotionally), I just couldn't do it anymore.

I thought that I couldn't voice my thoughts and opinions because it was a silent rule that women needed to be quiet and soft spoken, and I was not those things. I had opinions on how things could be run better in the house, but I was just too afraid of being judged or stepping out of line to voice them. So I stayed quiet and let that fear build. I saw how decisions were made in the group and I disagreed but felt obligated to accept them rather than to speak out.

For example, one person paid everyone's bills. We combined everything. We had one bank account for the entire house. I remember leaving my tiny room and seeing some of the bills get paid while ours got overlooked. I heard, "He can't get taken away to jail for unpaid bills." (referring to Brad) It made me so angry. We couldn't even pay our own bills. I had no control over my life. The feeling that someone else is controlling every aspect of my life was eerily scary. I was numb and couldn't think for myself. I hated it.

Within about five months of being involved in our community, I was approached about 'giving' my car to a couple that was leaving the land for good. The conversation went something like "Hey, 'so and so' are leaving and they helped us save for the land; and so we want to give them something to leave with, and we think it's best to give them your car." In my quiet and bitter heart, I agreed. I wanted to say no. I paid cash for that little black car with my hard earned money before I ever moved here. It was the only thing that was truly mine and I was being asked to give it away. I agreed because I felt like I couldn't say no. I was too afraid to say no. Not in a fearing-for-my-safety kind of way, but I had never let my real voice be heard and I wasn't about to let this be the first time. I signed over the title.

As I stared out the window and watched my friends driving away in my car that I resentfully gave away, I became pissed! So much anger was building up inside of me, and I didn't know how to get it out. I hated the lack of control that was taking over my life and I didn't know how to escape it. But I had to continue to live—I had no choice. The baby I was carrying saved our lives. I felt that no one would care if I took my own life, but I couldn't bring myself to take an unknown life as well, especially the one I was nurturing inside of me.

That season of our lives only lasted seven months, but it felt like an eternity. It got to the point where everyday I would tell Brad how sad and depressed I was; that this was not what was best for our lives and to please consider moving back to Maryland. I had to plead my case for our baby and myself. This was not how I envisioned raising a family. If we wanted or needed anything, we had to ask the main person in charge for money and permission to use a vehicle. That's how my life was run—by someone else. On some days it felt as if I couldn't breathe and I walked around feeling suffocated because I was so stressed.

After a few months of exhaustedly telling Brad every feeling and emotion that I had, he finally made the decision that we would move back to Maryland. However, we had no place to go and nothing to go home to. But we knew we needed to go. We moved back to our hometown and in with his parents. When we left 'the land,' we borrowed his parents' Jeep Grand Cherokee. It was filled to the brim with every last of our belongings that we owned. We had $200 cash and that was it. This felt like it was the real beginning for us. I felt like I was free. Although the shame and guilt of leaving our friends behind was so heavy, the freedom of leaving was refreshing. I was able to be me and become the kind of mom I wanted for our son. My spirit was relieved and felt lighter. The one thing I did get out of that season of my life was how not to be. This was one of the biggest lessons of my life. I learned that it is perfectly okay and right to want to live a life that I love and that I am proud of. I learned a ton of what *not* to do, which sometimes is better than understanding what to do.

Moving back to Maryland was one of the best decisions we could have made. The love and support we received from Brad's family was incredible. Not once did we feel judged for our decisions. His parents truly love with an unconditional heart whether they agree with the decisions we made or not. That made it that much easier to return home. We began to build our life on a solid foundation this time.

Shortly after we moved back to Maryland, we had Abel. He was beautiful and the most glowing baby boy with a perfect round head. I loved everything about him—especially that he was all ours. It was very healing for me giving birth to him and to know that I was now in control of my life and living the way that I wanted to. I was beginning to love my life and myself. This was new for me.

It was a lengthy process to forgive myself, my past and the people that were involved in my life that had hurt me. I harbored bitterness, anger and resentment for a long time.

Those feelings don't just go away on their own. They were the things that I would constantly work on and constantly ask God for help to get rid of. I don't remember a defining moment of when it all went away; but the more whole I became, the less I was consumed by holding onto to those things that did not make me a better person or make me happier.

ACTION STEPS:
- ✓ Identify which areas in your life you might be white knuckling and resisting.

- ✓ Understand that it takes a lot of courage and strength to be able to identify and accept what your circumstances are in your life.

- ✓ Write down the things that you are battling with or the things that you are scared of or desperately trying to change.

- ✓ Identify what is the worst thing that could happen? Foreclosure? A relationship break-up? Losing a job?

- ✓ Accept the reality of the worst case scenario. How would you feel? How would you move on and rebuild? For a few moments, feel as if the worst-case scenario happened. Imagine yourself in that situation and how you would get through and recover.

THREE
UN-FORGIVENESS

Refusing to forgive will hold us back from being successful in every single area of our lives. With un-forgiveness comes a plethora of other nasty emotions and begrudges. Un-forgiveness mainly hurts you, not the one you need to forgive. When I looked at my own life and realized that I had people who I needed to forgive, it wasn't fun. Here was what was in my mind and what might be in yours as well:

"Oh, I don't need to forgive. They were so mean and awful that they don't deserve my forgiveness."

"I have already forgiven them, but I am sure waiting for them to come to me and apologize—I bet that will never happen, though."

Those thoughts are laced with bitterness, pride and resentment. I unknowingly knew it well. You see, I thought I had forgiven and moved past them. But my day to day thoughts about certain people were far different from those of someone who had forgiven, healed and moved on in a healthy way.

One of my biggest misconceptions about forgiveness was that the other person would just 'get away' with what they did. In some ways we can think un-forgiveness will protect us, that if we forgive wholeheartedly we will be saying that the offense that was against us was okay and validated. But that is not the truth of it.

Forgiveness doesn't excuse the behavior. Forgiveness prevents their behavior from destroying your heart.

Nearly ten years later I saw that I still had up my walls of un-forgiveness to protect me from any more pain and abandonment.

Who do you need to forgive? Unless you have already worked through your forgiveness, I am going to help you identify it. What I don't want you to do is gaze. By 'gaze,' I mean I don't want you to try really *really* hard to 'find' someone who you need to forgive. I remember someone in our church asked me during prayer if there was anyone I needed to forgive. "Anyone? Anyone at all?" He asked. "Are you sure?" I felt badgered! Like *oh my goodness* if I don't figure out who I need to forgive I won't live life to the fullest and everything will be ruined and I will die miserable. Please.

God is the God of restoration and there isn't anybody or anything that can ruin that. For me it took God revealing it to me. At that time I honestly didn't see that I had refused to forgive anyone, even my mom. But if you know your heart is clean and you have forgiven those who have hurt you; you will be free and not carry around the weight that un-forgiveness takes. It's a part of life that everyone has been hurt at one time or will be hurt in the future. This happens knowingly and unknowingly.

Here are signs of un-forgiveness:
- Tendency to blame others
- Irritability or easy frustration
- Emotional exhaustion
- Repetitive sin habits
- Feeling like you have to prove yourself to other people

If you can relate to any of these habits then you might have un-forgiveness present in your life:

- Rehearsing speeches (I am guilty of this one!)
- Holding negative thoughts towards someone
- Avoiding a relationship/contact with that person
- Secretly hoping for retaliation
- Doubting that you can truly be happy for others when good things come their way

In 2005, I had a moment with God about my dad. I thought I had forgiven him for not providing for our family and being the role model that I needed in my young life. The confusion of being six years old and not understanding what was happening with my family was devastating.

As I sat there praying, I envisioned myself carrying my dad and laying him down at the foot of the cross and forgiving him. I was 23 at the time and knew that laying him down meant that I was releasing the anger, bitterness, sadness and disappointment I had toward my father, and I finally forgave him and gave him to my Heavenly Father. Even after that vision, I still didn't have much of a relationship with my dad. It was as if he was a stranger to me. I tried to write a letter here and there, but nothing really grew from my inconsistent attempts.

In 2008, it was as if I woke up out of bed one day and was in love with my dad again. I *HAD* to go see him! (He lived in Colorado and I was still in Maryland.) I felt this urgency and told Brad I had to do this. By myself. I took action and booked my flight. I couldn't understand why I felt the way that I did—it was like a switch.

At this time of this all happening, my dad was in the hospital. I was able to talk with him on the phone, although I could not understand what he was saying. He had just come out of surgery. I told him that I loved him and I asked him to hang on and recover because I was coming to see him. I cannot understand what happened to me, but all I knew was that I needed to see my dad. I needed to tell him I love him and ask for his forgiveness for not being the daughter to him that I could have.

I imagined caring for him and brushing his hair and just sitting with him. I had no other motive but to just love him.

I know this was God working in me because the abundant love I had for this man that had emotionally abandoned me didn't make any sense at the time. My dad never reached out to me and asked for forgiveness. He didn't apologize and try to make things right after all those years. But I forgave him anyway and I wanted him to know my new love for him.

My flight took off at 10:28 am. I was to fly to Phoenix and have a layover and then fly into Colorado. I had a great flight and sat next to an amazing woman who sweetly gave me half of her delicious turkey sandwich. I look back and remember asking God if I could sit next to an angel. I was excited for this journey and knew anything was possible! When I arrived in Phoenix I turned my phone on to call Brad to let him know I got there okay. I had six messages. The first one asked me to call my uncle. The second one was from my oldest brother telling me that Dad had passed away at 10:26 am that morning. I fell to my knees as tears and sadness poured out of me. I was confused and desperately asked myself if I could somehow figure out the formula to go back in time. I had to. I needed to tell him that I love him!

"Wait, *no*! I didn't get to tell him! I didn't get to tell him!" I cried out through my tears and heartache.

I sat in the airport on my knees for what seemed like days. I was raw, emotional and totally alone with more sadness and heartbreak than I have ever experienced. I am amazed at the kind people who stopped to see why I was sobbing. They had genuine hearts and shared my brokenness and vulnerability while in the most fast-paced place on earth.

A security guard came to me because people had reported a distressed young girl by the moving walkway. He walked me to the terminal to figure out what flight I could take home.

I was on a mission to see my dad that came to an abrupt halt of which I had no control over whatsoever. I asked God, "What do I do next?" And I heard him say, "You are doing it."

I was obedient to go see my dad. I wasn't angry that it didn't work out exactly how I had pictured it. I had no other choice but to go with it and figure out how to get home to my family.

The work of forgiving my dad had already been completed. I would have never been able to forgive myself if he had passed away and I was sitting at home on the couch. My presence in Phoenix was the only comforting thing to me, knowing that I was doing everything humanly possible to be with him. My mission ended earlier than expected and I was honestly okay because I knew God had worked things out so that it was best for me. I don't have any other explanation for it.

One of the most important things I learned was how people were open with me when they saw how vulnerable and raw I was. I did not hide anything. Every person I talked to would ask what was going on because I was wearing my emotions on the outside. I could not help it. It looked like I had been crying and starving for days.

People need relationships. Genuine relationships that are real, inspiring and honest.

That security guard who walked with me told me that his brother died unexpectedly and that he was angry. A gentleman

I sat next to in the terminal told me his dad had an affair out-side of marriage and he was so hurt to go through that. Then there was a man I sat next to on the plane as we were stalled on the runway due to weather (I was re-routed to Las Vegas to catch a connecting flight to Baltimore). He was a talker to the tenth degree!

When he asked if I was going to Vegas to party with my friends I simply said, "No". He then asked, "Well then, what are your plans when you get there?" Despite the tears running down my cheeks, I told him that I was on my way to see my dad and he passed away before I could see him, and now I was try-ing to get back home to my kids and husband.

He was shocked and speechless. This stranger began to have a great amount of warmth and condolences. He then be-gan to tell me his life story and then some. The man told me about his past, about his work and all about his relationships; I learned that he had three stepdads and could never commit to a woman because he had been badly hurt in his past relation-ships. I began to encourage him and tell him that all things will work out for our good, even in the most painful times.

I realized that this man sitting next to me felt safe enough to tell me things he had never told anyone else before. He saw how vulnerable I was. He was 65 and I was 26. His spirit connected with mine, and he felt that he could open up to me without any judgment. There is no other way to explain it. I felt God was using me to help this man in a way that maybe no other person had before. God knew I would be sitting next to this individual on the runway for hours at the exact moment that I was facing these distressing circumstances. At the time, I just wanted to grieve by myself and take comfort in my own quiet tears. But God had another plan for me, and that was meeting that man on the plane that I never got the name of.

And that woman I sat next to? Ironically, she was on her way to her aunt's funeral. She indeed was an angel. That half of her sandwich was the only thing I ate or drank for the entire 48 hours that I was being re-routed back to Baltimore. I couldn't stomach the thought of ingesting anything to eat or drink.

Un-forgiveness will eat away at you and can look like the following:
- Conversing with yourself in your head and asking yourself how to set a certain person straight, and how to get the last word in the conversation and be correct.

45

- Thinking, "I'm so sick of [Insert name here] thinking they are the best and that they have everything figured out."
- Thinking, "Everything always goes just perfect for them."

While ruminating on these phrases, did you think of anyone you need to forgive? I say these things only from experience. Bitterness is one of the consequences of un-forgiveness. Here's the thing about forgiveness—it is undeserved. We have been forgiven by a loving and tender Heavenly Father that we are undeserving of. Whether your God is the same as mine or not, you were forgiven before you were even born.

The person that wronged you may or may not have come to you and asked for forgiveness. Whether you choose to walk in and forgive them is up to you. Forgiveness is about setting you free from those emotions that are eating you away. Forgiveness is NOT for the person who hurt you; rather it is FOR you. Think about it: the other person isn't walking around worrying or wondering if you forgave them. But those thoughts that run through your head are laced with bitterness and are constantly thinking of that exchange that hurt you. This ultimately robs you from the fullness of the happiness that you are meant to have.

ACTION STEPS:

✓   Imagine yourself carrying that person to the foot of the cross. You lie them down and leave behind them and the pain that they have caused you. It is only out of *their* weaknesses and pains that they have caused *you* pain.

✓   You may need to revisit this and re-forgive if it was an especially difficult circumstance that you have trouble letting be. Just know that is normal. What you are doing by repeating the previous action step is creating a new habit to forgive when those feelings come up again.

I am very proud of you! This is the first step to becoming who you are designed to be and also who *you* deep down want to become.

FOUR
The F-Bomb

Brad eventually started his own general contracting business. We bought our first adorable little house and continued to grow our family. Life was normal and I was proud that we were making good decisions for our own family, which resulted in good things. In a few short years, Brad's business was thriving! We were making more money than we ever had, adding company vehicles, hiring employees and were able to do great things with the company. When we outgrew our first house with our growing family, we had three kids under the age of five. We needed to buy a bigger house. We did what everyone else does when you make more money. We upgraded to a bigger house. In order to sell our first home, we moved back in with Brad's parents. They are the most generous and loving people we know and we love them dearly. I have learned so many great lessons from them and we wouldn't be where we are today if it weren't for their love and unconditional support.

We listed our house and started to save for a down payment for our new house. When it came time to buy, we did what most of the population does. We bought the best house the bank would allow us. The first house we bought was $119K and the house we were saving for was $435K. We bought at the top of the market and the top of Brad's company. We were so happy! The first night of settlement we slow-danced on the back deck in the dark with the stars as our night-lights. There was no one anywhere near but the two of us. We were living our happily ever after and I couldn't believe our dreams were coming true. It was one of the most incredible and satisfying feelings I had ever had. It was only going to get better. We were going to make even more money and be even happier! We were able to pay off every red cent of credit card debt before we moved. It was the ultimate freedom! We were so happy to own over an acre, four bedrooms, two and a half bathrooms, a two-car garage and a finished basement. We never needed to move again if we didn't want to, and we really liked that.

I would go grocery shopping when I felt like it or had a craving for a dinner idea. I would pick up clothes and shoes when I was out and didn't really have to think about the money I was able to spend. I would stock up on big sales and use coupons for things we didn't really need. Life was perfect and I felt so accomplished that we 'made it.' We had everything that we wanted. We were unconscious of the amount of money we were spending. It's not like we lived in a mansion, went on luxury vacations or drove a Mercedes. But we were comfortable.

When the checks would come in, they would get spent. We were not good stewards of the money we were entrusted with. The money was going out as fast as it was coming in. We did not have authority over money. The money had authority over us. We did not govern it the way God had intended money to be managed.

Through many challenges and seemingly hopeless situations, we were taught very tough lessons. Life slowly started to unravel this seemingly oh-so-well put together life. With the crashing market and fall-out economy, Brad's company rapidly declined as fast as it grew. We were living off of credit cards and struggling to pay our bills and feed our three kids. We used our savings for gas, food and minimum payments on our credit card bills. Our electricity was even shut off for a time. We were *that* behind.

My life sucked. I was lost. I had no idea how we were going to get out of this mess. I was convinced that I was one of those people that God could care less about and that He had abandoned me and my family. Just like I thought He had abandoned me during my childhood and while living on 'the land.'

The days turned into weeks and then into months of constant struggle and hardships. We were making it and still breathing—but just barely. I was desperate to help our situation any way I could. Brad's company came to an end and he went back to his old boss...*again*. There wasn't enough work in the company to get a full 40-hour work week. Sometimes his paychecks would be less than $500. I would have to count how many more checks we needed to come in just to pay our $3300 mortgage alone. We were beyond living paycheck-to-paycheck and drowning fast. When the company ended we still had business debt that we were responsible for. We were facing the idea of bankruptcy and foreclosure not only on our home but also on a rental property (our first home never sold, so we rented it out). We were going to lose everything if something didn't change.

After borrowing money on our credit card just to fill up my gas tank, I had a slap-me-in-the-face moment. I knew I had to face my fear of leaving the kids to go to work. The ability to provide for them, clothe and feed them was bigger than my fear of going to work nights while Brad worked days.

My life was falling apart. I did not deal with it well. Like at all. I did not have the character or maturity or faith in God to be able to endure the pressure cooker that I was in. I had three young children with no ability to help Brad provide financially for our family. I felt stuck as if I was buried in concrete. The crash of the market, Brad's business and my life was over as I knew it. It felt as though the earth would stop rotating and we would literally fall off of it. I didn't care how Brad and I would make it. But I cared deeply about how we would provide for the kids, answer questions about how our life was changing and how I would have to face the fact that I let each of them down.

I would fall asleep at night feeling the weight of my world sinking me deeper and deeper. I felt ashamed and irresponsible. I felt so dumb for having ended up with this wreck of a financial situation. It seemed like there was no way out. Not even for us.

I ended up applying for a serving position at a new restaurant that was opening up. I was the first person in line with my application in a manila folder, and I was dressed to land this position at a high-end restaurant. The general manager pranced in late with her drive-through coffee in hand and wearing a starched pant suit. I was terrified. We really needed the money and I was so worried that I wasn't good enough. After two rounds of interviews I ended up getting the job, and I felt so incredibly blessed because I was not qualified and had no experience. This was the beginning of a sliver of hope for us. We began to really look at our finances to figure out how to get out of this mess.

Before I was blessed with my new job, we were dealing with financial trouble, marital stress, and creditors calling multiple times a day and coming to our home with court papers. They were set with court dates for Brad (most of our credit cards we loaned to the company were in his name) to attend. They also said it would result in a warrant for his arrest if he failed to appear. My days were overtaken by stress, depression and anxiety. We were so far behind on our bills I never knew it could be taken to the serious level it was getting to.

I would cry out to God, "Why is this happening to us? Why are you allowing this?" I was convinced that He could care less about what we were going through and only cared about the people who came from cookie cutter families. I felt as though He was so angry with us for making our mistakes and this was His way of getting back at us. Through emotions of anger, bitterness, hopelessness and complete failure, the days still went on and on. We did not starve, go to jail or lose our houses. But I was mad. I was mad at God. I was angry with Brad and mostly completely let down and disappointed with myself. I felt like a complete failure. How could I let our financial situation get to the point it was at? How could Brad not provide for us the way he was able to in the past? Why was God okay with us going through this? After all, we thought we were following what God wanted us to do. How could this happen if you are on the right path? I drove myself crazy. I became so anxious and stressed that it was manifesting physically in my body. I was diagnosed with ulcerative colitis. I was bleeding where people should not bleed. The stress levels that were on Brad and I were unbearable. To be honest, I didn't think we would make it out of this—especially together. This was the most difficult time in our marriage. With each passing day, Brad and I would say goodnight and tell each other "We made it through another day." That tiny victory of making it through each day alive and together was what kept us going.

I share these stories of what we went through to give you hope. Whatever you are going through is figure-out-able. As long as you have the breath to face each day, you can get through anything. Draw upon the strength of your Creator to see you through the tough times. It just took me a while to real-ize all along He was right there with me. My perspective of God was completely false. He is for me and not against me. He cares deeply about what is happening in my life and what I'm going through. I just didn't believe it at the time. Through all these devastating times the best thing that happened to us was that our characters were being molded and strengthened. We chose to put up a fight and not get taken under by the pressures of the stress. We came out on top by choice, not by luck! It would have been easier to file bankruptcy and not pay our mortgage. At times I wanted to do that. But I knew that we were meant to fight this. Even as hard and hopeless as it seemed at times, it was for our own good and we would be blessed.

It wasn't until I took responsibility and faced my fears that things started to turn around for us. Slowly but surely things were changing; and I had to accept the situations in my life. I was angry and I fought tooth and nail in order to deny it. As much as this made me feel abandoned and like a failure, I had to accept this as my reality. I wasn't going to give in. This wasn't going to overtake my family or me. I would come out with victory, not defeat!

I had to face the fact that we could potentially lose everything: our houses, our money and our dignity. I imagined how we would climb out of those worst-case scenarios and still be okay. We would have scrapes and bruises, but we would be okay. I want the same for you. You will be okay and you will make it through. No matter what you are facing, as painful and unfair as it is, you can face it. It might be the scariest thing you have ever done. Yet, there is nothing stronger than the human spirit.

Coming to a point where you cannot control certain aspects of life means throwing your hands up and not taking on something that is impossible for you personally to fix. Surrender those things in your life over to God. If they are out of your control, what better thing to do than to give them to a loving God who *is* in control of it?

I had to realize that some things were just simply out of my control. I liked to think that I was control. But I was not.

The things that were in my control were my only responsibility, and I tried to do the best I could.

This is a prayer that I still pray often:

Dear Heavenly Father,
I thank you for bringing me to this point. I thank you for this crossroads in my life. Right here and now I hand over to you _____. It is not mine to stress over. I freely give this over to you. Thank you for being the guiding power in my life. Please help me to remember to continue to hand this issue over to you and not take it back and try to fix it on my own. I am expectant and excited to see how you will work this out for the good on my behalf because you love and adore me.

-Amen

During the times that we had money coming in, we didn't know how to keep and grow our money. When we made plenty we would spend it on our house, trucks, shopping, furnishing the house and—to be honest—I couldn't even remember where it all went. We learned how to manage money with the toughest lessons to learn.

I am going to show you how to save more money, pay off your debts faster than you thought possible and make your money work for you. We learned this by almost losing it all.

Break your budget down to three categories:
• Giving/charity
• Savings
• Obligations

If you don't set intentions with where your money should go, it will vanish into thin air. Ever say to yourself, "Where did all that money go?"

We've been able to pay off multiple thousands of dollars in debt doing these action steps. This time we have learned the principles and laws of how money works. Follow these action steps and you will see a dramatic difference in your bank account in no time!

ACTION STEPS:

✓ **Identify the NEEDS** – This might be hard, but really look at where your money is going. If it is an absolute then keep it; if you aren't sure, then consider what life would be like without it.

✓ **Discipline yourself** – Nobody cares more than you do about your bank account. The next time you are in a store and have something in your hands that you feel you need to have, disciplined yourself on saying 'no.' After a while you will feel empowered that you are so strong and that you are sowing seeds that will be multiplied later.

✓ **Cut the junk** - Go through what you are spending money on each day—coffee shops, eating out, gym memberships, alcohol, cell phone contracts, internet, cable. This will hurt. But what would you rather have, money in the bank or stiff pressures of debt and an empty bank account?

✓ **Look at you interest rates (and not the good kind)** -This one is the most important! Look at your credit card statements. Look at how much you are being charged just for the luxury of borrowing the bank's money. That will wake you up! Look at the interest, the interest rate and the fees. That $19.99 sale is now jacked up to over $50 or more by the time you pay it off. (depending on your credit card interest rate)

✓ **Automatically save** - Did you know 28% of people don't have any savings*? Set up an automatic savings plan. Even if it is only $5, DO IT. Increase it later when you can. Along with paying off your debts, you must have money in the bank for the inevitable future bumps in the road. *(http://money.cnn.com)

✓ **Downgrade** – In a world full of up-sells, upgrades, bigger and better, think about what you could downgrade in. Think about your car(s), house, cell phone, etc. Take the money you keep from those other expenses you canceled, and pay off debt or put it into savings. Seventy-six percent of people are living paycheck to paycheck. (http://money.cnn.com)

✓ **Pay it off once and for all!** – Make a list of all your
credit card and loan debt. Start with your lowest balance
and pay it off as quickly as you can. You will feel so empowered that you have taken a stand on your debt and
have control *over* it instead of sinking under it. Once
that is paid off, start on the next highest balance.

You will soon realize that you can actually work towards
being debt-free; you just didn't realize it because you didn't
have a plan. Your money is meant to be seed for you to sow.
When you sow seeds of discipline and faith with your finances,
you will be entrusted with more. Money is meant to work for
you and not hold you in bondage.

We have to get smart about our finances! It dictates
everything we do, who we can help and how we live.

There is a reason that wealth is mentioned over 250
times in the Bible. There are principles that teach exactly how
to acquire wealth, keep it and use it for good. But we have to be
willing, teachable and disciplined to obey. When talking about
money, some people will quote the verse "money is the root of
all evil" when taking about being wealthy and having riches.

When we were in our most devastating financial times I can honestly say I loved money. I thought about it all the time, I worried and stressed over it. And it caused evil in my life. But the verse actually says "For the love of money is the root of all evil." (1 Timothy 6:10) Money is neither good or bad. It is a tool that we need to use in our lives. Whatever position we place it in our lives is up to us.

Acquiring financial knowledge is a skill. It is something that is learned. You would think that we were financially free when we were making the most money we had ever made. But we were still living paycheck to paycheck. It does not matter how much you make; what matters is how much you keep.

We are all groomed in a certain way regarding our finances. Are you trying to have the best and biggest to keep your ego jacked up? Are you the kind of person that is dead broke and spending money on beer with your friends who are also broke? We have a responsibility to grow our income so that it can be used to serve others.

Think about the people you know who are wealthy. Maybe you used to think like me and think people like that were greedy and just lucky. In reality, those are some of the most successful, generous and loving people. Why? They have developed skill sets in this area. I do not mean to ruffle feathers. You may be the slim part of the population that cares about bettering yourself and knows wholeheartedly that you are here to make a difference in whatever avenue that is. You want to shine bright so that other people want to become better simply because they see in you that it is possible. I applaud you. It wasn't easy to learn the things I am teaching you. When I would read or hear things that would offend me, I would recognize that I clearly had more to learn and that was the reason I was offended. It was something that I didn't know.

I have a question for you. I want you to answer it honestly—no holds barred. What is that teeny tiny voice that is whispering inside of you? That thing which is an idea or a business or something you would do cartwheels if you could actually make money doing it? Are you stuck in your job and desperately trying to figure out a way to make extra money? Think about that random idea that has crossed your mind. Who do you think put them there? We were designed to serve people with the natural gifts and talents that we were created with.

Some of the most successful people I know are so crazily passionate about the 'work' because their income is a coming in from their natural gifts and talents. God didn't create us to be average. He didn't make us to barely get by. We were created to excel!

I want you to write down that 'thing' that is a whisper—or maybe it's even louder than that. What is that one thing you could do to take action? You have to be willing to move forward. God is waiting for you to step up and be bold and courageous. If you are worrying what people might think, move past that fear.

It is only an idea in your head. Who cares what your best friend, co-worker or relative thinks? What have they done in their life that is so spectacular that they are in a position to judge you? This is about YOU stepping into the destiny that has already been set in place. It is a mandate to bless you and people through you. That feeling within you to go further and deeper is GOD-given. You did not produce that on your own. It is from Him. It is a gift. That thing is meant to change the world, whatever it may be. Maybe you were given an amazing idea for an app that will make people's lives easier, or you are an artist and inspire people through your art. What are you doing to step into your gifts and talents? Are you increasing your skills to master them?

Think about what motivates you. What makes you excited? Whatever your answer may be, there is something there that is calling your name to move forward!

I could go on and on. I encourage you to step into the fullness that God has to offer you. But beware—it may look completely different than what you thought. In the later chapters I will go more in-depth about developing your natural skill and sharing your own story to earn profits.

If you haven't stopped by BarbaraDiane.com, come on over and introduce yo' self! You'll want to enter your email for the stuff I only talk about in my emails.

FIVE

When Life Hands You The Unexpected

(a.k.a. Shit Sandwich)

As dumb as it may sound, I thought that when we moved into our overpriced, ego-building, forever house we were 'done.' Meaning, we were done saving for a down payment and paying off debt (we were credit card debt free but didn't have skills to keep it that way), and we were making a great salary collectively between my part time gigs, Brad's income and a rental property. But in reality, it was just the beginning. Being over our heads in mortgage payments, eventually in credit card payments, and suffering through a steep decline in business.

Although our dumb ass decisions were allowed by God, they may have been the very thing that He used to draw us to Him on a deeper level. There isn't anything we can screw up so badly that will permanently derail us from greatness! God is so much bigger than that!

You see, I adored Brad. He was my everything, my provider, best friend and lover. Looking back, I realized I had placed him on a pedestal. He was my comforter and could always make everything better. I relied on him for my happiness and fulfillment. Yet when my life seemed to fall apart, my trust and faith in Brad was shaken. This needed to happen because then the only thing I had left was God. I did not realize that Brad was #1 in my life, which is not the way God intended a marriage to be. God finally became my #1 after I shook my fists and pissed and moaned over our struggles. The very place of pain was the place of gain, comfort and protection. God showed me that He will always provide for me and never forget me. No matter how bad I had screwed things up, I still was looked after. What I was going through mattered greatly to Him.

Remember when I told you I had gotten the job that I wasn't qualified for? Well, I excelled at my position (which I will talk more about in the later chapters). I was then offered a full time management position. I would have gotten benefits, great health insurance and a steady salary. Even though I was terrified of working so much and balancing time with my family, I decided to go through the interview process with our corporate headquarters. I was scared to even accept the invitation to interview. But I did and I was grateful for the opportunity. I was climbing the corporate ladder, which I never thought I'd be good enough to do. But this was the direction that my life seemed to be taking.

I interviewed for the position and waited to hear back. In the meantime, life carried on. A day before I found out that I did not get the position, I also found out that I was pregnant! I could not believe it. It felt like God was playing a joke on us. We had just gotten to the point where we were climbing out of the hole we were in. It seemed like the most irresponsible time to bring a child into the world. Yet, it was happening.

I had to choose to be joyful and positive. I could not allow myself to worry and be anxious and think of all the reasons why it was not the best time to have a baby. I knew that God had a plan—a plan that I couldn't begin to understand. And for some reason I made the choice to trust it.

We had prevented having another baby for four and a half years, not sure if we wanted to add another child to our family and NOW I was pregnant. I wasn't very good at entirely trusting God with my life. But in this moment, I knew very well that I needed to trust Him in order to get through this in one piece as well as to keep my family's emotional state in tact. I was not willing to become a lunatic of a mom because I was worried to death over how this was going to work out.

We were climbing out of over $50,000 in debt. We struggled to get ahead with two incomes. In nine months we were going to drop back again to only one breadwinner.

What has happened in your life that made you realize that things were out of your control? Maybe you have lost everything? Maybe you are desperately trying to have a baby? Did you lose a loved one sooner than you ever expected? Those things suck. We may not understand in a timely manner or even ever, but God plans everything to work together for the good of those who love Him. He says so. Whatever is out of your control creates an opportunity to hand it over to a Heavenly Father who wants to bare it all for you. It is a test. All God wants for us is to love Him. That is the number one command. Love the Lord your God with all your heart, all your might and all your soul.

When we have complete trust in Him, we fall more and more in love with Him. One cannot fall deeper and deeper in love without fully trusting with their entire being and every human need and soul. See how He works? He allows things in our lives to happen even when they look like the death of us. He has a plan and all we need to do is surrender ourselves back over to Him.

Things will happen in life that are so painful, so trying and simply not understandable. But the *way* we react to them determines what is waiting for us on the other side of that 'thing.' I believe that every person has a 'thing' that is a spot of pain and struggle. Maybe that 'thing' is your finances like it was for us, or you just can't find a decent human to date or your family's health history seems just so incredibly unfair. Most of the time that is the area that you need to completely surrender to, let go of and be happy and content even if things don't work out exactly how you want them to. Could you see yourself being okay with things turning out differently than you previously hoped for?

It's okay if your answer is a big fat no, but I want you to consider that 'thing'—that area in your life that you have not completely surrendered to God.

ACTION STEPS:

- ✓ Write down what your biggest struggle is that is out of your control.

- ✓ Make a commitment to yourself and to God that you will do your best to trust Him. That's all he wants from us, and it is the best we can do. He is so understanding and knows when we are trying our best.

- ✓ Read this prayer that will help guide you through the process of surrendering your 'thing' to the One who was meant to bear it.

Dear Heavenly Father,

I thank you for bringing me to this point in my life. Right now I surrender _____ to you. Please forgive me for trying to figure everything out and control it. I was created to trust and love you and right now I am choosing to give this to you. It is yours to work out in my life and I trust and believe that you will do the very thing you promised me. You will work things out for my good because I love You. I come to you with childlike faith and lay this down at the foot of your cross.

- Amen

SIX

Get Out Of Yourself

One way to help solve our own problems and issues is to help others with theirs. When we are so focused on ourselves and what we have going on, there is no room in our hearts and minds to even consider what someone else is going through. We were each created with a servant's heart. Think about how you feel when you help someone and they are so thankful and appreciative. It feels *so* good, doesn't it? It feeds our soul when we are used in a way to bless others. If serving others is not part of each of our lives, *we* miss out on blessings for ourselves. I'm sure you've heard the verse in Acts 20:35 that it is better to give than to receive. If we only think about ourselves, we cannot be used to bless other people because we are not open to anything but our needs.

Don't get stuck in the rut and misconception that you will help when you *eventually* have the time, the money or the energy. Give encouraging and loving words. Give whatever you can give *now*—even if it's only a few bucks or giving time to volunteer somewhere. When we can give a little bit we will be given more.

There are so many people who are worse off than you. No matter what you are going through, someone else has it worse. Use what you have been blessed with and help someone else. You will feel fulfilled in a way that only happens when you give and help others.

After Brad and I left 'the land,' we began going to a small church that met in the pastor's house. Every Thursday we would have WIP, which stood for worship, intercession and prophecy. One Thursday night we had a big family of visitors. They had never been there before. During our prayer time, it wasn't uncommon to get a prophetic word for someone and openly share it. Opening up and sharing what God was pressing on my heart at the time was new to me—especially in public. As the violin strings were playing in the background, I felt such a heaviness and burden in my heart for this family. I couldn't explain it. I began to share with them that I just felt the heaviest sense of burden for them. It felt as if we were mourning the loss of someone, almost as if someone had just died! I placed my hand on a man's shoulder who was probably in his mid-twenties. I began to speak words of love and encouragement for this family and I said that what they were going through was not too big for God to heal. I felt like God wanted me to tell them how much they were loved. I felt so vulnerable and nervous to share what seemed like such dark and emotionally heavy things with this family that I had never met. But the power of the Holy Spirit was so strong that I didn't doubt its truth.

About two weeks had passed since that night, and I found out that this family had begged their son to come to the meeting that I spoke at. That man that I had rested my hand on was planning to commit suicide that night. He had his gun by his nightstand and was ready to carry it out after he got home. He never did. That night changed the outcome of that man's life. I had no clue! I was just openly praying and sharing with this family what was in my heart. But if I hadn't let down my guard and forgot about what I sounded like and refused to share, the outcome for that man could have been different. God had a message of hope for that family and He chose to speak it through little ol' me.

God chooses to show His undying love for us through people that we encounter everyday. You have so much to offer people. God has given you authority, love and a powerful voice to show love through many different ways.

ACTION STEPS:

- ✓ Brainstorm the ways that you can get out of yourself and serve other people.

- ✓ Starting today and over the next few days, look for an opportunity to bless and help someone out. Whatever that opportunity may look like, it will create a new habit to think more outside of yourself than what you are used to.

SEVEN
Default VS. Design

When I came to the realization that I was unhappy and my life looked nothing like I had thought it would be, I began to really search my soul, (as cliché as it sounds) for my purpose. "God isn't a very good God if *this* is all that I am going to be," I thought. But the truth is that my choices were what landed me in my position of default. My choice to be miserable, scared and anxious led me to a level of depression that I never thought I would get to. I thought I would just end up being something great! As naive as that sounds, I believed it. I grew up with the misconception that *because* I was a Christian, God was just going to help me have a wonderful life. EEEH. *Wrong!* Although that is His heart for everyone, there are so many factors that come into play when it comes to the way we handle our life.

I would see non-Christians having super happy and fulfilling lifestyles even though they weren't serving the God I thought I knew. These were the people who didn't believe that Jesus died for them and who don't confess their faith to God. (Looking back, I judged the people who I thought didn't believe like I did. Yuck. Who am I to judge someone's heart?) I felt jipped. Why should I serve God anyway if I'm going to be this unhappy? What's the point? I needed to stop trying to prove that I had a right to be the one He created me to be and start ACTING like it! It wasn't just going to happen simply because I was breathing. The truth is that I was serving my fears and *myself*. This leads to ultimate misery and depression.

God is not a respecter of persons (James 2:1-13). The laws of success are what make people happy. I am not just talking about monetary success. I am talking about the law of reaping and sowing. No matter what your belief in God is you can sow positive thoughts by serving and loving one another.

What you give you will receive, whether you believe in the most High God or not. It's truth and it's His laws. I thought the purpose of serving God was receiving what I could get out of the deal—what He would do for me because of my commitment to Him. But in reality the purpose of serving God only comes after we realize that we are reflecting back to Him the great love that we receive from Him. He first loves us and when we see that, we can't help but return it back to Him and other people. It's a natural love cycle.

So here I was soaking in my own negative thoughts, poverty mentality and completely self-centeredness. I was reaping all the negativity I was feeding my mind. Whether or not I was a Christian or not had nothing to do with my circumstances. It had everything to do with what I was doing with my life, my thoughts and my actions. I take complete responsibility for it. Until we take responsibility and make the notion to change what we have done over and over, nothing will change. Ever.

The point I want to get across is this: Wherever you are in your life, it is because you allowed it to happen. I want you to think in a sense more of where you are mentally, emotionally and spiritually. Then look at where you are circumstantially. At the point in my life when those areas were dark and depressing, my circumstances lined up completely with that. Some of you reading this are humble enough to accept it. I was angry once I truly accepted that where I was in my life was because of me. I will say that even though my husband had the same circumstances as I did, he was still happy. He was still positive and hopeful. He knew it was just for a season of time and we would come out of the hardships we were facing. I chose to be negative. I chose to be hopeless and allow anxiety to take over and manifest physically in my body.

There is a destiny planned out for you that was set in place before you were born. It is not God who withholds greatness from us. It is ourselves who do not allow His greatness to flow from within. There is a plan set to prevent you from reaching your destiny just as there is a plan set in place for you to reach it!

"Be still in My Presence, even though countless tasks clamor for your attention. Nothing is as important as spending time with Me. While you wait in My Presence, I do My best work within you: transforming you by the renewing of your mind. If you skimp on this time with Me, you may plunge headlong into the wrong activities, missing the richness of what I have planned for you. Do not seek Me primarily for what I can give you. Remember that I, the Giver, am infinitely greater than any gift I might impart to you. Though I delight in blessing My children, I am deeply grieved when My blessings become idols in their hearts. Anything can be an idol if it distracts you from Me as your First Love. When I am the ultimate Desire of your heart, you are safe from the danger of idolatry. As you wait in My Presence, enjoy the greatest gift of all: Christ in you, the hope of Glory!" (Jesus Calling, Sarah Young)

DEFAULT: The default part of life that we all can fall into is accepting the mediocre. God didn't design us to live a mediocre life; he designed us to excel! If you are going to your job, hating every second of it and always looking toward the weekends, that is settling for mediocrity. Getting home from work and plopping down in front of the TV everyday isn't what you were designed to do. We can be mediocre in everything. Our thoughts, our decisions and lifestyle.

If you are living for the weekends then you are dying in the middle of the week. When you go to work, put a smile on your face and be the best you can be at whatever position you are in at work or business.

DESIGN: If you knew you couldn't fail, what would you go after? What is the 'thing' that is burning in your belly that you would just love to do with your life? Chances are, that 'thing' is what you are meant to pursue as a way of serving people. I encourage you to go after it! You only have this one beautiful life. If you don't pursue it, whose fault is it for not accomplishing it? Yours. We have to be willing to take the first step. When we take the steps, God takes two with us. In the Great Book it is mentioned over 350 times to do not fear. If it's mentioned more than once, it's probably really important. You will get bumps and bruises by following your 'thing,' but you will learn from it and be okay.

ACTION STEPS:

✓ Find ways to grow yourself. Network with new people, and read books that will improve your life. The more you grow and stretch yourself, the happier and more well rounded you will become. The happier and more well rounded you become, the more you will attract like-minded people and opportunities will come your way!

81

✓   Make a list of the things you've always wanted to do. Take that hike, go to your local winery, etc. Make new habits. We can all get stuck in the routine and humdrum of life. You will feel refreshed and will look for more creative and fulfilling ways to spend your days.

✓   Look at what you are sowing. A good indicator to see how you feel about what you are *sowing* is by looking at what you are *receiving*. What are you receiving relationally? Financially? Emotionally? Spiritually?

✓   Make a conscious decision that you will change your thoughts and the way you feel towards situations and people.

✓   Pursue those passions that are like a fire in your belly. We all have them. For some, you know exactly what it is, and for others it may have been buried for some time now. There is always an opportunity to rediscover what you were born to do. Could it be music? Business? Computers? Missions? You won't know until you step out and gain clarity. Figure out what makes you happy. If you are feeling heavy and saying to yourself, "Well, I guess I'll just do this," or "This is what I should do." Those are dead indicators that it's not the right thing for you.

EIGHT

Your Dream

What does your dream life look like? It's different for everyone because you have different desires from your parents or me. But whatever they are, you were meant to live them. They have been instilled in you by The Creator.

Remember back to when you were a kid? You imagined what your dream job would be. You dreamed of your dream car, spouse, house, job, vacations, etc. And as you got older, your dreams might not have come to reality. As you started working and paying bills, your dreams had to diminish to fit within your budget. What are you willing to do in order to reach your dreams? Maybe you need to cut your hours back at work or your business in order to spend precious time with your beautiful family. Maybe you are called to missions in another country and you just aren't sure how you can make it work. Maybe you need to drastically cut your spending to get out of the pressures of debt. My purpose in writing this book is to serve people and help you change your life. Sometimes we need another person to point out what we already knew in order to gain a different perspective.

God wants you to dream again. Dream your dreams once more. Your dreams should be so BIG that you can't achieve them on your own. If you can do them on your own, they're not big enough. Dream big dreams, include The Creator of the universe and get to work. With the proper actions and a little amount of faith, incredible things can grow! Faith without action is just dead and crappy.

What holds most people back—including myself—is fear. This is fear of the unknown, fear of success, fear of other people. It can be fear of just about anything.

Definition:

Fear - **anticipation** of the **possibility** that something unpleasant will occur. (dictionary.com)

Let's break down the definition of fear. The word **anticipation** means to wait. The **possibility** which means could happen. So it's like saying you are waiting for something that could happen. See how unsure that sentence is and more so to live like that? There is no truth in fear. Fear is rooted in pride and ego. The fear of not putting yourself out there could drastically affect *someone else*'s life. Yet, what if it does work? Your goal may exceed your wildest imagination and create a movement to change the world!

When I started in a internet network marketing business I was terrified. When I made my first video I felt like I was going to puke, all because of the fear of what people might think. I had no clue what I was doing. All I knew was that I wanted to succeed. I had a burning passion inside of me and I was determined to pursue it. I would be a fool not to. What did taking action do for me? With every step I took in business, I got closer to where I was meant to be. With every phone call I was nervous to make, every blog post, every video and training webinar, I learned how to improve and increase my skills.

You cannot succeed if you do not invest in your skills. The market place pays for the skills you have. Lack of skills equals lack of income. Increasing your skills means you are automatically increasing the amount of money you will get paid. This means increasing your people skills and increasing your knowledge in a certain area that you are good at. Master a brand new skill. When I left my job as a restaurant manager and started searching on the Internet, I knew NOTHING. I had ZERO skills and had no clue what I was going to do. But I was coachable, humble and open to learning new things. Open your heart! Just by being open and available, brand new opportunities can come your way! It will look like hard work. But I encourage you to step up and into what very well could change your life forever.

Have faith! Faith is the key to opening up new blessings that God wants to give you. Let's look at two different types of people:

First type: Everyday they wake up and their first thoughts are negative—they dread going to work. They are miserable inside and out. They are the 'bah-humbuggers' who think that nothing good will ever happen to them and that good things only happen to 'those kind of people' that come from golden sperm. It's almost like they are expecting and waiting for things to go wrong. This was the exact kind of person I used to be!

This type of person is sowing negative thoughts, which means they are reaping negative things in their life. Negative people remain in negative and hopeless situations and are not thriving in anything.

Second type: This type of person wakes up expecting great things to happen. They are happy to be breathing and to be able to go to their job. They count their blessings, which makes them glow on the inside. This type of person knows deep down in their gut that they were meant to do more with their life and serve more people. They are pleasant to be with and do the best they can with what they've got. This person is sowing faithful thoughts and actions that will eventually reap more blessings and favors in their lives.

Which one do you think will be in a position to receive a blessing and more positive opportunities? If you have children then think about these two as kids. One has a nasty attitude and one has an easy, obedient attitude. Which one would you want to bless? Person number one can't see all the blessings that they

already have and person number two is actually opening themselves up for more abundance!

Which one are you?

Answer that question honestly and you will immediately open up yourself to what you may need to change in your life. Don't be discouraged if you are in fact the first type of person and then some. This is the beginning. No one can change anything without first recognizing where they are—myself included. The goal is not to strive to be perfect. That's how we will drive ourselves insane. We will mess up and we will disappoint. The goal is to make small increments to reach a better self. Next time the kids get crazy, try handling them differently. Next time you are going to eat out of comfort or convenience, grab something healthier and feel good about yourself. Next time you didn't get the outcome you wanted, find the one thing that you can focus on that's positive instead of instantly focusing on the negative.

If you are just starting out, you will not know everything you need to know. But from my experience, I realize that everything will come to you when the time is right and when you are ready for it. The most important thing is that you start. Start small and scale up. Don't wait for everything to be perfect and be in place just so, because it never will. I remember being in the hospital with my fourth baby and studying the ins and outs of my business. I was determined to succeed come hell or high water! Sometimes my persistence drives me nuts, but I know that it was given to me to be used for a purpose. The more I can persist, the more people I can help. I learned from Dani Johnson that the more successful you become, the more influence you will have in the marketplace and in your network. If you are struggling in certain areas of your life, how can you help others who are struggling? You were created to excel! You were created to serve others with your heart, love, wisdom and God-given talents. You can do that my friends! YOU were created for more. Settling for less is in direct conflict with your design. God wants YOU to impact the world! Will you say amen to that? Whatever that may be in your life will look differently from the calling in my life. God has designed a custom plan for you! Be obedient and step out in faith. It will be so worth it.

ACTION STEPS:

✓ Begin to keep inventory of your thoughts. What you are thinking about most is what is manifesting in your life.

✓ Review the company you keep. Are the people you are surrounding yourself with the people you want to become like? You are likely to become like the five people you hang out with. (businessinsider.com) Are you okay with becoming an average of them? Please don't be afraid to change your environment and friends if they are weighing you down and not helping you become who you are meant to be.

Nine
The Hidden Truth

This may not mean much to you if you are a man. But it could improve the way you view women and their roles. I grew up with my single mom. She worked because she had to provide for six children. She did not enjoy working as hard as she had to, but she did so in order to provide for us. As I grew up I had a PASSION and deep desire to be a successful businesswoman, but feeling that way made me feel so guilty. It was always the *quiet rule* that women need to stay home and raise their children while the husband works. This especially applied to faithful Christian women.

Before I go any further, Brad and I decided that I would stay home and raise our kids. We wanted to make that choice. I didn't want to put them in full-time daycare and miss their milestones. I did not have a career to come back to after having our first baby. But I had these underlying rules in my head of what it looked like to be a Godly woman. I'm sure some guilt made part of our decision, too. Everything is hindsight, but when I had my first son I thought that women should stay home and home school, bake, do crafts and clean. And if that is what makes your heart skip a beat, then do that. However, if it's working outside the home then do that. Don't get wrapped up in the should or should nots. You will go crazy. As always, have balance. Being a workaholic and never seeing your kids is no good either. Figure out what would be your happy balance and do your best to make it work, regardless of what other people may say or think of you. Being a mom is hard enough. Let's support every mom out there who is making the best decisions for her family. It only makes us feel worse when we sense dis-approval or judgment by another mom who does things differ-ently than we do.

Have you ever felt like you *lost* yourself as a woman after you had kids? I know I did big time. I remember the way I felt after I had my third child. After waiting for my husband to get home so I could get out by myself. I anticipated my alone time all day with enormous amounts of excitement! I ended up feeling so vulnerable and alone in the store. I didn't know what my style was anymore, I didn't know what I liked. I felt naked without a baby on my hip, my diaper bag and my husband along side of me. After years I had lost touch with myself. I didn't know who I was without my little people and responsibilities. This was a huge wakeup call for me.

I didn't want to be the woman that after 20 years of raising my kids I finally give myself the time of day. I realized I had to take baby steps to nurture myself and listen to who God was calling me to be as a woman, apart from my mom role.
In the Bible there are so many POWERFUL women that exhilarate me!

Take Lydia for example. She sold purple garments to the most wealthy. She was rich and a businesswoman. In order to get the fine dyes and cloth, she needed to purchase those materials first before she could make things from them to sell for profit (Acts 16, The Message Bible).

Deborah, judge of Israel, is another great example. She was the only female judge who was famous because of her wisdom and courage. She had the authority to order Israelite warrior Barak to take 10,000 troops to kill Sisera. Not only was she a wife, but she was also a prophetess. She prophesied that a woman would kill Sisera. And indeed he was killed by a woman! (Judges 4, The Message Bible)

Last but not least, we have the infamous Proverbs 31 woman. King Lemuel's mother describes a virtuous woman to be her son's wife. So this guy is a KING, and this is who his mother says would be suitable:

A wife of noble character who can find?
She is worth far more than rubies.
Her husband has full confidence in her
and lacks nothing of value.
She brings him good, not harm,
all the days of her life.
She selects wool and flax
and works with eager hands.
She is like the merchant ships,
bringing her food from afar.

She gets up while it is still night;

she provides food for her family

and portions for her female servants.

She considers a field and buys it;

out of her earnings she plants a vineyard.

She sets about her work vigorously;

her arms are strong for her tasks.

She sees that her trading is profitable,

and her lamp does not go out at night.

In her hand she holds the distaff

and grasps the spindle with her fingers.

She opens her arms to the poor

and extends her hands to the needy.

When it snows, she has no fear for her household;

for all of them are clothed in scarlet.

She makes coverings for her bed;

she is clothed in fine linen and purple.

Her husband is respected at the city gate,

where he takes his seat among the elders of the land.

She makes linen garments and sells them and supplies the merchants with sashes.

She is clothed with strength and dignity;

she can laugh at the days to come.

She speaks with wisdom,

and faithful instruction is on her tongue.

She watches over the affairs of her household

and does not eat the bread of idleness.

Her children arise and call her blessed;

her husband also, and he praises her:

"Many women do noble things,

but you surpass them all."

Charm is deceptive, and beauty is fleeting;

but a woman who fears the Lord is to be praised.

Honor her for all that her hands have done,

and let her works bring her praise at the city gate.

-The Message Bible-

Now that is one rockin' woman! I want to be just like
her! She's strong, makes an income for her household, she's
blessed, has maidservants who help her, raises her kids, speaks
with wisdom, fears the Lord and her husband stands behind
her, supports her and calls her blessed. How inspiring is THAT?

Although, I do think there is a side note to mention
about this 'woman'. I don't believe that this woman was changing diapers, nursing, starting a business and on top of everything at the same time. Just as our lives change in seasons so do

our goals. As women, wives and mothers we can't be everything all at the same time. So I don't want you to feel overwhelmed if you are barely getting a few hours of sleep with a newborn keeping you up at night. I used to feel ashamed that I wanted to be more than a mom and wife. I couldn't shake the fact, however, that I also had these deep passions that really excited me. After surrendering these passions to God, I finally became free by realizing that He had given me those desires and my voice. I don't care what it may look like to other people. I care that I am following the calling on my life and desires that God had planted within me. I am only accountable to God. He is the judge to whether I listened to Him or not—whether I obeyed and pressed forward or not.

What I am about to say are my fighting words. Get off your religious soapbox. Many of you may be offended by this. But I know you are a person who wants more truth in your life.

Don't let your religion hold you back from fulfilling your destiny. Don't let yourself be held back because it doesn't look like what a 'Christian' would do. BLAH! *YUCK*! Do you love God? Do you hold Him in your heart and give Him glory? Then go do that 'thing' that is constantly whispering to your heart! He is asking you to obey that. Will you? I grant you permission to fulfill your calling. Sometimes all it takes is for someone to encourage you to be YOU and not what people think you should be or do with the life God gave you. God will move mountains if you are obedient.

As you step out in faith, He will be behind the scenes working things for your good. Ask your spouse and children for their support and understanding. Brad is 100% supportive and my biggest cheerleader. He believes in me and has the utmost confidence in me. I wouldn't be where I am today if not for his unconditional love and support and him picking me up when I've failed big time and have fallen flat on my face.

TEN

10 Principles For Success

God certainly set boundaries in place in order to help and protect us and help us succeed in our lives. The word 'if' is said multiple times over and over in the Bible. The word 'if' is dependent on what is done. For example, you will be successful with your bank account IF you are trustworthy with the money you have. You will live a healthy lifestyle IF you eat, clean and workout. Opportunities will come your way IF you are willing to step out. It's a condition. It probably ruffles feathers to use IF and God in the same sentence because we think that God just does and is. I know *I* did! He sets up boundaries and His principles for our betterment. Once I learned these truths, they rocked my world! I can do these things! It takes discipline and new habit-forming ways, but they are simple to follow.

PRINCIPLE #1: FORGIVENESS

This is the most important law. Forgiveness. This is a daily action that we must continue to grow in. It is imperative to know if you want to grow and move forward in your life. When we do not forgive we are acting out of bitterness, which is just nasty behavior. Forgiveness keeps us from resenting people and the past and gives us the key to live in faith and have favor with God. Forgiveness brings life and freedom. No wonder it is part of the daily bread prayer:

Our Father in heaven,
hallowed be your name.
Your Kingdom come,
your will be done,
on earth as in heaven
Give us today our daily bread.
Forgive us our sins,
as we forgive those who sin against us.
Lead us not into temptation,

but deliver us from evil.

For the kingdom,

the power and the glory are yours.

Now and for ever.

Amen.

One guarantee in life is that people will let us down and disappoint. Sometimes we have nothing to do with actions that are done against us. But we have everything to do with how we react and if we choose to forgive. Un-forgiveness will rob you of creativity and open opportunities. Forgiveness is not about letting people off the hook so that they can get away with what they did. It is for you, your freedom and the generations of blessings to be a legacy you leave your future generations. Forgiveness is a daily choice.

ACTION STEPS:

✓ Think about those people who you thought of while reading this are most likely the people you need to forgive.

✓ Don't think of everyone and anyone. You will go nutso! Think about the ones that are evident who you must choose to forgive if you want to be free in every area of your life.

✓ Remember that un-forgiveness holds you back. It does not accept or justify the other person's behavior.

✓ Try out this prayer for forgiving those who have hurt you.

Dear God,
Please forgive me for holding un-forgiveness towards
_____. Thank You for forgiving me for my faults. Today, right now, I choose to forgive
_____. I lay them down at the foot of your cross. You are the one who is to judge them and not myself. I want to be free and clear of any bitterness so that I may be clean and grow into who I am meant to be. Please help me to walk this out daily.
-Amen

PRINCIPLE #2: Vision
You must have a vision for where you are going.

If people can't see what God is doing,
they stumble all over themselves;
But when they attend to what he reveals,
they are most blessed.

(Proverbs 29:18, The Message Bible)

Most people 'wait' on the Lord to drop a duffel bag of money on their front step or to win the lottery so that *then they can do something significant for the Kingdom of Heaven.* That just isn't how He works. He is searching for those who are faithful, diligent and ready to step up. God says that He will light your path. Do you know where you are going?

Work unto the Lord in what you are doing right now. In your job, in your home, raising your kids, whatever it is, work for The Lord.

As I was talking with my then seven-year-old daughter, Destiny, she asked me what I thought she should be when she grows up. I responded by telling her whatever she wants to be. She then said, "Yeah, but I want to be what you think I should be." Although I love her loyalty to my opinion, I wanted her to trust herself enough to make that decision on her own. She *already* is who I want her to become—my daughter.

She wanted me to name things she could be. I said she would be a good teacher, dancer, stylist, singer, etc. She wanted me to narrow it down to which one I thought would be the best for her to become. I tried to reassure her that she has the freedom to choose what she wants and sees as best.

That conversation with my daughter was a situation that mirrors what we do with God. We ask Him what we should do or become, and the truth is that we already are who He wants us to be. We were created. God wants us to be happy and choose what we want to do. What makes Him happy is when we use our brain and make good decisions. Just like a *real* parent would.

Imagine if you were buying a car and asked God what color you should choose. He would probably say, "Which color do you like?" Then you might say, "I like the black one." To which he may respond, "That's a great choice! You should get the one you like." God is not going to be driving the car—you will. See how natural God is? He is real. When we do our best in every situation and decision - in our natural life - God's super-natural collides and miracles begin to happen!

ACTION STEPS:

✓ Write down your goals and where you want to be in the future. Brad and I wrote down our one, three, five and ten year goals. They can be anything. Don't hold yourself back if they seem silly. For some of you this might be uncomfortable, but do it anyway. Don't limit yourself or God!

✓ Pray over them. Ask God to help you and guide where you are going.

✓ It's okay if you are afraid. You are human. But the most important thing to remember is to not let fear hold you back from taking action. Remember, faith without any action is dead!

PRINCIPLE #3: THE MIND
Be transformed by the renewal of your mind:

Thought = Actions = Results.

Different thoughts = Different Actions = Different Results

Are you still thinking the same old way? I promise you this. When you start to think about your life and situation differently, you will act differently and have different results.

If your daily thoughts of feeling inadequate and the fear of never having enough or failing are always on your mind, your life will become exactly that of your thoughts. By replacing those thoughts with what your Creator has said about you, life will gain a new perspective. Sounds cheesy, but when you catch yourself speaking words of death to yourself (which we all do), instead replace those thoughts with words of life!

Thoughts of death
- "I can't afford that."
- "I don't have time."
- "I'll never be able to do that."
- "I feel stuck."
- "It's so hard to..."
- "Nothing ever works out the way I plan."
- "Everything always works out for _____."

Thoughts of Life

- "I am good enough."
- "I have something very special that the world needs."
- "I can figure out a way."
- "I can make time."
- "My needs are always met."
- "My worth is valued by who God sees me to be—not by my clothes, friends or money."
- "I can do this."

When you begin to think differently, you will act differently. Your circumstances will change. But they can ONLY change when you begin to change your thought patterns and habits.

ACTION STEPS:

✓ Reflect. What are you grateful for right now? Are you the bah-humbugger? No one else gets to choose your mindset and perspective for you. You get to choose. Isn't that cool?

✓ Change your thinking to serve you instead of burdening you.

PRINCIPLE #4: VALUE

How valuable would you say you are as a person in your job/business? Could they replace you in a heartbeat? What determines your value is the amount of skill you have. Are you a highly trained brain surgeon? Are you a retail clerk? The brain surgeon obviously earns a higher salary because they are required to have more skill for their vocation.

The only person who is responsible for their skill is themselves. So the more skill you invest in yourself, the more the marketplace (people) will pay you for your job/service.

Also, think about this: When you walk into your job, are you ready to work with a great attitude or are you strolling in with your phone while checking those last few posts on Facebook? Which type of behavior would you say your employer sees as better work ethic? How's your attitude when you are at work? I got promoted at my last job because I didn't get involved with complaining and gossiping. I was there to do my job and I did it with a cheerful attitude and great work ethic. Like I previously said, I was not the best. But I had that leadership factor that my boss was looking for when it came time to promote someone. I brought more value to the workplace than the other employees. I am not saying this to brag, my behavior was the reason why I was promoted over the others.

ACTION STEPS:

- ✓ Ask yourself how you could increase your current skill and make yourself more valuable to your job or business.

- ✓ Ask yourself how you can adjust your attitude or work ethic to become the go-to person that your boss will want to promote.

PRINCIPLE #5: REAPING AND SOWING

This one is my favorite and I would say the second most important! It's a no brainer. What seeds are you planting? Think of seeds as thoughts, financial spending, time management, serving and positive speaking that you are sowing. You will reap exactly what you have sown. If you waste your time doing dumb things, you will always feel like you never have enough. The same is with money. If you keep doing the same damn thing and repeating bad choices hoping for a different outcome then that is the definition of insane!

You already know if you need to mend relationships for a different outcome. You already know if you need to lose weight.

You already know when you need to make a change in your life to get a different result. The question is are you ready to make that change for the outcome that you *really* want? I know this may be coming across as tough. But I mean it with love and encouragement. Changing the areas that are damaging in your life starts with a decision to make that change.

ACTION STEPS:

✓ Take responsibility for your current situation. It is not until we take responsibility for our actions that we can change anything.

✓ Evaluate the things that are coming into your life. Are you attracting abundance and more great things or is one decision after the other making life harder?

PRINCIPLE #6: DESIRE

You bought this book for a reason. You are a person who wants to better your life! You have a God-given desire to be the best you can be, right? The desires that you have reveal your destiny. You were designed for greatness and to succeed. But life's ups and downs groom us to believe that we are meant to fail. I thought I was born a failure. The truth is, however, that everyone is born with gifts. It takes discipline and persistence to bring them to the forefront. It is people who don't believe they are meant for anything special or have enough worth to succeed. The solution to that is to change the way you think!

Start thinking that you are successful. Start treating your relationships as if they are valuable to you and protect them. Quit believing that you are always going to be broke. Stop whining and complaining about everything and anyone. You will amaze yourself as you watch yourself become the person you were meant to be.

ACTION STEPS:

- ✓ Start valuing the desires of your heart. Protect your dreams. The world needs you to step out into your calling. It's going to be scary. You may lose a friend or two, but it will be okay.

- ✓ Begin to respect the natural gifts you possess. You may feel bad about being extremely talented in an area or really good at something. It's okay to own it! It was a gift that has been given to you and it's your responsibility to bless others with it.

PRINCIPLE# 7: COACHABILITY

It wasn't until I was in the darkest place in my life that I became teachable. It was an aha moment of "Holy crap! I have no clue what I'm doing. I need help!" I began to learn from other people who were living the way I wanted to live. They had solid and loving relationships and were changing the world with the voices that they were given. Are you coachable? Are you willing to learn from other people who have figured out areas of life better than you have? You will need to shed your pride and ego. I did. I had to in order to get out of the mess we were in. Ego will sound like "Well, I don't have that problem," "I can figure it out on my own," or "What will my friends think of me?" Your ego will tell you to blame everything and anything. Your ego will disguise itself to keep you stuck. There is nothing that makes satan happier than preventing you from doing what you are meant to do.

ACTION STEPS:

- ✓ Find someone who is where you want to be in life and ask them how they did that! Begin to learn from other people and follow their leads.

✓ You must be comfortable with being uncomfortable in order to change your life. When you learn a new way, take action and put it into place to make it a strong habit that will serve your life and eventually others.

PRINCIPLE #8: Promotion

Every successful person that I have studied has always said the following:

"It's never the circumstances that determine your success in life, but rather how you *deal* with the circumstances that determine your success in life."

When Brad and I went through our worst time financially as we dealt with creditors from business loans, working full time day and nights, *and* dealing with our fourth pregnancy. This was the scariest time in my life. We were struggling to pay for our house, bills and support a growing family of five. I knew I had two choices of how to deal with it: I could be positive and hopeful or resent my situation and crumble. Most days I wanted to die under the covers and would wish it would just all go away. But the fighter in me was determined to make the best out of this *blessing* that was coming at a time completely not part of *our* plan. Which I am forever grateful for. Isaac completely re-routed my life and because of him I was forced to make different decisions.

How are you responding to the circumstances in your life? Are you dealing with them the best that you can? I have a feeling that you want to deal with them even better than you have been already. This is for your benefit.

I learned that I needed to prosper where I am planted. That means if you are a stay-at-home mom, you are caring for your beautiful kids and keeping a great attitude while doing the laundry, grocery shopping and cleaning *again*. If you are a corporate executive, be that person that inspires and encourages the employees below you. Be the one who shows up to work and does the job with a cheerful heart and a great attitude.

When we are faithful to where we have been planted, we will be given more. It's God's law! If you feel like things are just not going the way you have wanted them to, you could be going about life the wrong way. Don't press and push things to happen. Be content and faithful, and you will be given more—more time, more money, better relationships and more influence.

ACTION STEPS:

✓ Take one day at a time and do the best with what you have. Wherever you are, there is always a way up. You will be promoted when you have mastered the art of gratitude with your current circumstances.

✓ Don't worry if you feel like your boss or anyone else doesn't notice how hard you are working. God sees your heart and your work ethic and nothing gets past Him, ever! He loves to reward and bless!

PRINCIPLE #9: FOCUS

You will do well in whatever you set your mind on daily. Do you want to get better at the things you are focusing on? Are you focused on things that you are lacking? Or are you focused on abundance and gratefulness? Listen. You do not have to go around life skipping and barfing rainbows in a picture-perfect world in order to be in a state of happiness and joy. Sometimes in my hardest days I have needed to reset my mind to think of all the great things in my life. It is a habit. I am re-training my brain and forcing it to think positively and not negatively. The more you do this the better you will become at it. It will develop into a skill. When I first started doing it, it was difficult just like any other new habit. But it became easier with practice. When I caught myself in a crappy mood or my thoughts going in a downward spiral, I would remember that I have control over my life and it was my choice to continue or to change it.

Focus on what you want to get better at, no matter what it is for you. You could be striving to become a better mother, a better employee, or a more caring friend. Don't beat yourself up if you are just now realizing all of the bad habits you have formed. People don't know what they don't know, right? For example, you will act differently if your thoughts are always telling you that "there is never enough." If you train your thoughts to think, "I always have enough and all of my needs are met," then you will act differently—I promise. I say this from first-hand experience.

Work towards progress, not perfection. We are all human with our own faults. The goal is not to strive to be perfect; that's how we drive ourselves insane. We will mess up and we will disappoint. The goal is to improve in small increments to reach a better self. Find the one thing that you can focus on that is positive instead of instantly focusing on the negative.

ACTION STEPS:

✓   Take a minute and think about what you focus on a daily basis. If someone were to go into your head and write down everything that you were thinking and focusing on, what would it look like? Would you feel happy about the results or disgusted by the garbage you have allowed yourself to take in?

✓   When you catch yourself thinking negatively and focusing on things that will not make you better, change it. You only have control over one thing and that is YOU. You control your thoughts, reactions and choices. The more you are able to shift your thoughts, the stronger you will become and easier it will be to change your thought patterns.

PRINCIPLE #10: TEAR DOWN THAT IDOL

When I first started learning about idols and how powerful they are, I was broken and humbled. There is a reason God says, "Have no other idols before me." I thought that only crazy people had idols or other things that they worshiped other than God. I knew back in biblical times that their idols were little wooden statues. And I felt utterly disgusted with myself that I had built up a greedy, selfish and prideful idol of money.

Some of you may think that only rich people are greedy and idolize money, but I can assure you that we were not rich. I was fearful of providing for our family. I was scared to death of the future and how we would make it. I was anxious about keeping our employees employed. Every day I would check the bank statements to make sure that we didn't go over. I prioritized our finances higher than my Omnipotent Heavenly Father. I still didn't trust Him to provide, which goes to show that it doesn't matter how much you make.

As much as we were making, I still worried about money. It was a difficult issue that He wanted to work out in me. God knew exactly where my fear was coming from and used that fear to teach me to trust Him.

I had created a bigger place in my heart for fear, anxiety and worry over money. I was a professional worrier. These things were my idols and it must have saddened God that I would place those things in a bigger part of my heart over Him. I didn't even realize what I was doing! I had put so much energy and passion into serving those disgusting and ultimately death-ly 'gods.' I chose whom I was serving and it wasn't God Himself.

What or who are you serving? Are you so focused on your body image that every thought and action about it is over-taking you? Are you so focused on meeting the 'right' one that you drive you and everyone else around you crazy? Are you so worried about other people's opinions of you that you would rather be approved by them than by God? Are you too focused on your health and constantly fear that God will never heal you? An idol is anything we prioritize higher than Christ alone. This may be a difficult issue to accept, but just know this. We have a loving, understanding and compassionate God. He knows what we do and what is inside our hearts. But that doesn't stop Him from loving us completely and wholly.

ACTION STEPS:

- ✓ Repent. Change your daily thoughts with a complete 180. It's really simple. When we see an area in our life that has become bigger than it should, we need to release it.

- ✓ Learn this prayer that will walk you through how to re-pent:

Dear Father,

I repent for_____. Please forgive me for making _____ more important than you.
Thank you for your love and understanding. Please help me to
walk this out daily and make you my focus and main priority.
-Amen

ELEVEN

Passions Into Profits

Every single situation, challenge and season of your life has brought you to this point. You are right where you need to be. It may not make sense now. It may not make sense ever. But just know that behind the scenes in our lives there exists the ultimate designer and creator who works all things for the good of those who love Him. You can't go back and wish you could change things. I encourage you to not waste any time or brain cells focusing on those regrets—that will only depress you. Have faith; have hope knowing that you are right where you are meant to be. For some of you, that may seem like a really crappy place. Bear with me, and I say this with love. There are things that life wants you to learn. Ask yourself, "What can I learn from this?" Have you been in the situation you are in before? How did you end up there? Most of the time when we don't learn our lessons the first time, life has a funny way of bringing it back around and with an even greater force. We are meant for greatness and not mediocrity. But we have to choose to step up and be wise with our lives, decisions, relationships, finances, etc.

You Are Meant For GREATNESS!

You were not meant to scrape by and struggle. God definitely uses those situations in our life to bring us closer to Him and to teach us how to be better. But He has plans to help you prosper and to give you the future you hope for! I love this passage from the Bible:

When you call on me, when you come and pray to me, I'll listen.

When you come looking for me, you'll find me.

Yes, when you get serious about finding me and want it more than anything else,

I'll make sure you won't be disappointed. God's Decree.

I'll turn things around for you. I'll bring you back from all the countries into which I drove you...bring you home to the place from which I sent you off into exile. You can count on it.

Jeremiah 29:11

Many of you might be disappointed with your life right now. The message that God wants me to send to you is that you are right where you need to be. *Exactly* where you need to be, in fact. You are in the right job, born into the right family and going through the proper struggles that you are facing. He uses these situations all for the good of those who love Him. You are gaining strength and character, and you are learning how to deal with life's let-downs so that you can be equipped for the next season of your life.

Even if it sucks right now, it won't always. I do believe that we have to do our part and our best. Some things are just out of our control and there is nothing we can do about them. But the issues that we do have control over need to be dealt with using wisdom and love. Things are being worked out in your favor behind the scenes. Whether you realize it or not, whether you even care or not, God is helping you. There isn't anything that God can't or won't turn around for you. He just loves you that much! There isn't anything that is too big for Him.

You may feel like you don't matter too much. But you matter to Him more than you'll ever know. He knows every fiber within you; your DNA was his idea. I say this because it's the truth. Honestly, most days I can't even wrap my head around the amount of love He has for me. But it's the truth. And when our spirits hear truth, it sets us free. He loves you and wants you to be the best you can be and to live out your dream life. He is your biggest cheerleader, encouraging you to be all you were meant to be. God is a rock-star who will help messed up, screwed up, broken and shattered people. If He will use a DONKEY to speak through, don't you think He could use us? In the Bible there are characters that engaged in wild sex stories, murders, wars and filth, but God used *those* kinds of people to bring good to His people and the world.

What He wants you to know is that you have a unique voice and passion that no one else can offer this world. And this world is hurting a lot right now. Would you agree? We need you to step out in faith and do, create and speak up. Be the person that God designed you to be and whom you secretly wish you could be!

Think about ways that you can create a product (such as an ebook, video series or coaching program) that could help and serve someone else. What experiences have you been through that you can help others get through the same thing?

For more coaching on this topic check out www.BarbaraDiane.com

Whatever you do please don't undervalue your life experiences. I thought the things I went through were just a waste of time and would never mean anything significant in the long run. Little did I know that they would be used to help other people. Those things I went through would be the very thing that would be used to design and enter me into my destiny and calling.

One thing I learned about humility is this: **True humility** is accepting the truth about who God says you are. If you were put in charge of something you had no experience with and felt completely inept, and yet they still wanted you for that position, it would be so humbling! That's how God is with us. True humility is accepting who God designed us to be. We are His mouthpieces in this world to share His greatness. We are the ones in charge of showing HIS love. *Gulp*! That's a huge responsibility! But he gave it to us anyways; even though he knew we would fail at times. But he loves us so deeply that it doesn't matter. He wants us to depend on Him for our needs—personal needs, financial, mental, etc. He is a loving God who knows *way* more than any of us combined.

I will leave you with this. No matter what stage you are at in life, just know that God is not done with you. His work within you is a daily and life process. You mean the world to Him and he won't let you down! Ever. Put your trust in Him to see you through your challenges and pain. If you have been given a huge vision for life, take action by starting with baby steps towards it. When God sees that we are faithful with what we have and recognize the gifts he has given us, doors will open up for us.

Don't give up hope on your dreams or your circumstances. If I would have given up hope this book would not be in
front of you. I believe in you. I know that you have the Creator
of the universe backing you. Go out and be great, it *is* His will.

Words from my heart to you:

You are beautiful.

You are worthy.

You are designed to excel.

You are fully equipped.

You are destined for greatness.

You are qualified.

Most of all you are loved.

It has truly been an honor to share this book with you! I
am grateful for the chance to be a part of your life in a small or
big way. I look forward to getting to know you better and learning how I can serve you more. I am excited to see how God is

working out miracles in your life! Please share with us any insights you have discovered from reading this book.

If you haven't already joined our Facebook community, come say hi and introduce yourself!

Http://www.facebook.com/BarbaraDianeOnline

Lastly, remember that this world needs YOUR special gift that only you have to offer!

Your voice matters. Change the world with it.

Attention Event Coordinators: If you are considering booking Barbara Diane to come speak to your group, conference or special event. Please email admin@BarbaraDiane.com to discuss special circumstances, arrangements and fine tune material.

Ordering Information: Quantity sales, special discounts are available on quantity purchases by corporations, associations and others. For details contact admin@barbaradiane.com

www.ingramcontent.com/pod-product-compliance
Lightning Source LLC
Chambersburg PA
CBHW052112090426
42741CB00009B/1782